Little One

Nejla Ali

ISBN
978-1-5437-4662-4 (sc)
978-1-5437-4663-1 (e)

Print information available on the last page.

To order additional copies of this book, contact
Toll Free 800 101 2657 (Singapore)
Toll Free 1 800 81 7340 (Malaysia)
www.partridgepublishing.com/singapore
orders.singapore@partridgepublishing.com

06/28/2018

PARTRIDGE

To Minnah Fatima
For the lucky parents of girls.

It's your turn, little one,

Your turn to go into the world.

'What is this world?' you ask.

It's a place of wonder,

A place of learning,

A place of *mischief*, and a place of *yearning*.

Mischief: playful misbehaviour, especially on the part of children.

Yearning: a feeling of intense longing for something.

Where the sun brings light, and where the moon brings night.

You will take love with you; you will take happiness.

For the lucky ones who will get to know you, you will take a mind filled with thoughts and a heart filled with *knots*.

There will be some who will make you smile, and there will be some who will make you mad.

Knots: fastening made by looping. Knots can also be what your heart feels when your happy, sad, angry, anxious etc. Like an unexplained uneasiness which can be good or bad.

All will teach you, and all will help you grow; and because you are so smart, you will grow and grow and grow and grow.

It's time for you to go, little one, it's time for you to grow.

Your beautiful self will be a gift to the world, a world of beauty and wonder for you to know.

Now you know what you must do. Open your heart, and open your mind, but take care to ask, 'How are you today?' and, 'How can you I help you?' sometimes.

You know what you must do. Show kindness, show *respect*, but do take care, and don't forget to ask yourself, 'Are you happy? Are you your best?'

Live your best life because you deserve this beautiful world, and it deserves beautiful you!

Respect: a feeling of deep admiration for someone or something caused by its ability, qualities, or achievements.

Remember to speak true, speak right.

Remember to look and listen and only then to make up your mind. Your mind is a curious thing; it unlocks all the doors that are closed , it is the key to find you your glow.

'How?' you ask.

The more you feed it with books and learning, the more it will grow. And it will tell your body and *soul* to grow. It will say, 'Come on, then, now we know, knowledge and truth are the way to go.'

_____

Soul: the principle of life, feeling, thought, and action in humans; the spiritual part of humans.

Remember to take care of your body; love it just so.
Feed it nature's many gifts and sometimes chocolate
cake, ice cream, and marshmallows!

Ready then? Off you go!

Look out world, here comes-she,

Filled with sugar and spice and all things nice!

Love her, teach her, and treat her just right.

She is sent from heaven, a gift to make the world just right!

Printed in the United States
By Bookmasters